TRA ARMENIAN COOKBOOK

AVA BAKER

CONTENTS

APPETIZERS   1

EGGPLANT DIP (BABA GHANOUSH)   1
STUFFED GRAPE LEAVES (DOLMA)   3
CHEESE BOREK   5
LENTIL KOFTE (MERCIMEK KOFTESI)   7
SPINACH AND CHEESE PHYLLO TRIANGLES   9
EGGPLANT CAVIAR (IKRA)   11
HERB SALAD   13
YOGURT AND CUCUMBER DIP (TZATZIKI)   14
CHEESE AND HERB STUFFED MUSHROOMS   16
RED PEPPER AND WALNUT SPREAD (MUHAMMARA)   18

SOUPS AND SALADS   20

LENTIL SOUP   20
TABBOULEH SALAD   22
CUCUMBER AND TOMATO SALAD   24
YOGURT SOUP (MADZOONOV KHOROVATS)   26
BEETROOT SALAD   28
GREEN LENTIL SALAD WITH HERBS   30
COLD CUCUMBER SOUP (TZVIKA)   32
POTATO SALAD   34
MIXED BEAN SALAD   36
CHICKPEA SOUP (SHORABAT ADAS)   38

MAIN COURSES   40

STUFFED BELL PEPPERS   40

GRILLED LAMB KEBABS (SHISH KEBAB)   43

CHICKEN PILAF   45

VEGETABLE MOUSSAKA   47

BEEF KOFTA   50

STUFFED ZUCCHINI (KOUSA MAHSHI)   52

LAMB STEW (KHASHLAMA)   54

EGGPLANT AND CHICKPEA CASSEROLE   56

FISH KEBABS   58

LENTIL AND RICE PILAF (MJADDARA)   60

SIDE DISHES   62

ROASTED VEGETABLES   62

GREEN BEAN SALAD WITH FETA AND LEMON DRESSING: 64

PICKLED VEGETABLES   66

BULGUR PILAF WITH MUSHROOMS   68

CABBAGE ROLLS (KALAM DOLMA)   70

SPINACH AND CHEESE STUFFED BELL PEPPERS   72

HERB PILAF   74

GREEN BEANS WITH TOMATOES   76

POTATO KEBABS (KARTOFLU KEBAB)   78

SPINACH CASSEROLE   80

DESSERTS   82

WALNUT BAKLAVA   82

GATA (ARMENIAN SWEET BREAD)   85

RICE PUDDING (SUTLAC)   88

APRICOT AND NUT BARS   90

HONEY CAKE (TATIK)   93

WALNUT COOKIES (KURABIYE)   96

FRUIT COMPOTE   98

SWEET CHEESE PASTRY (GHURABIYE)   100

NUT BRITTLE   103
DATE ROLLS (RAHAT)   105

MEASURES   106

APPETIZERS

Eggplant Dip (Baba Ghanoush)

Servings: 4 Time: 45 minutes

Ingredients:

- **2 large eggplants**
- **2 garlic cloves, minced**
- **2 tablespoons tahini**
- **2 tablespoons lemon juice**
- **Salt and pepper to taste**
- **Olive oil for drizzling**
- **Chopped parsley for garnish**

Directions:

1. Preheat the oven to 400°F (200°C).

2. Prick the eggplants with a fork and place them on a baking sheet. Roast in the oven for 30-40 minutes until they are soft and collapsed.

3. Remove the eggplants from the oven and let them cool slightly. Peel off the skin and discard.

4. In a food processor, combine the roasted eggplant flesh, minced garlic, tahini, lemon juice, salt, and pepper. Blend until smooth and creamy.

5. Taste and adjust the seasoning if needed.

6. Transfer the dip to a serving bowl, drizzle with olive oil, and sprinkle chopped parsley on top for garnish.

7. Serve the Baba Ghanoush with pita bread, crackers, or fresh vegetables.

Stuffed Grape Leaves (Dolma)

Servings: 6 Time: 1 hour 30 minutes

Ingredients:

- 1 jar of grape leaves (about 40 leaves)
- 1 cup rice, washed and drained
- 1 onion, finely chopped
- 1/2 cup chopped fresh parsley
- 1/4 cup chopped fresh dill
- 1/4 cup pine nuts
- 1/4 cup raisins (optional)
- 1/4 cup olive oil
- 1 teaspoon salt
- 1/2 teaspoon black pepper
- Juice of 1 lemon
- 2 cups vegetable broth or water

Directions:

1. Rinse the grape leaves under cold water to remove excess brine, then drain and set aside.
2. In a bowl, combine the washed rice, chopped onion, parsley, dill, pine nuts, raisins (if using), olive oil, salt, and black pepper. Mix well.

3. Place a grape leaf on a flat surface, shiny side down. Trim any tough stems.

4. Spoon a small amount of the rice mixture onto the center of the leaf, near the stem end.

5. Fold the bottom of the leaf over the filling, then fold in the sides, and roll it up tightly into a cigar shape.

6. Repeat with the remaining grape leaves and filling mixture.

7. Place the stuffed grape leaves seam-side down in a large pot, packing them tightly in layers.

8. Pour the vegetable broth or water over the stuffed grape leaves. Place a heatproof plate upside down on top of the dolmas to keep them from unraveling during cooking.

9. Cover the pot and cook over low heat for about 1 hour until the rice is cooked and the grape leaves are tender.

10. Remove the dolmas from the pot and arrange them on a serving platter.

11. Drizzle with lemon juice before serving.

Cheese Borek

Servings: 8 Time: 1 hour

Ingredients:

- 1 package of phyllo dough, thawed
- 1 cup feta cheese, crumbled
- 1 cup mozzarella cheese, shredded
- 1/2 cup fresh parsley, chopped
- 1/4 cup unsalted butter, melted
- Salt and pepper to taste

Directions:

1. Preheat your oven to 350°F (175°C) and grease a baking dish.
2. In a bowl, mix together the feta cheese, mozzarella cheese, chopped parsley, salt, and pepper.
3. Lay one sheet of phyllo dough on a clean surface and brush it lightly with melted butter.
4. Place another sheet of phyllo dough on top and brush it with butter. Repeat this process until you have a stack of 4-5 phyllo sheets.
5. Spread a generous amount of the cheese mixture evenly over the top sheet of phyllo dough.

6. Roll the phyllo dough stack into a log, starting from one end.

7. Place the rolled log into the greased baking dish, seam side down.

8. Repeat steps 3-7 with the remaining phyllo dough and cheese mixture to make more rolls.

9. Brush the tops of the rolls with the remaining melted butter.

10. Bake in the preheated oven for 30-35 minutes or until the Cheese Borek is golden brown and crispy.

11. Remove from the oven and let it cool slightly before slicing into servings.

Lentil Kofte (Mercimek Koftesi)

Servings: 6 Time: 45 minutes

Ingredients:

- 1 cup red lentils, rinsed and drained
- 2 cups water
- 1 onion, finely chopped
- 2 cloves garlic, minced
- 1/4 cup olive oil
- 1/4 cup fine bulgur
- 1 teaspoon ground cumin
- 1 teaspoon paprika
- Salt and pepper to taste
- Juice of 1 lemon
- Fresh parsley, chopped (for garnish)
- Lettuce leaves (for serving)
- Cherry tomatoes (for serving)

Directions:

1. In a saucepan, bring the water to a boil and add the rinsed red lentils. Cook until the lentils are soft and mushy, about 15-20 minutes. Drain any excess water and let the lentils cool slightly.

2. In a skillet, heat the olive oil over medium heat. Add the chopped onion and minced garlic. Cook until the onion is soft and translucent, about 5 minutes.

3. Add the cooked lentils, fine bulgur, ground cumin, paprika, salt, and pepper to the skillet. Stir well to combine and cook for another 5 minutes until the mixture is heated through and the flavors are blended.

4. Remove the skillet from heat and let the mixture cool to room temperature.

5. Once cooled, shape the lentil mixture into small oval or round kofte balls using your hands.

6. Arrange the Lentil Kofte on a serving platter lined with lettuce leaves.

7. Drizzle the kofte with lemon juice and garnish with chopped fresh parsley.

8. Serve with cherry tomatoes on the side as a delicious appetizer or part of a mezze spread.

Spinach and Cheese Phyllo Triangles

Servings: 12 triangles Time: 1 hour

Ingredients:

- 1 package of phyllo dough, thawed
- 1 cup frozen spinach, thawed and drained
- 1 cup feta cheese, crumbled
- 1 cup ricotta cheese
- 1/4 cup grated Parmesan cheese
- 2 tablespoons olive oil
- 1 onion, finely chopped
- 2 cloves garlic, minced
- Salt and pepper to taste
- Melted butter for brushing

Directions:

1. Preheat your oven to 350°F (175°C) and line a baking sheet with parchment paper.
2. In a skillet, heat the olive oil over medium heat. Add the chopped onion and minced garlic. Cook until the onion is soft and translucent, about 5 minutes.

3. Add the thawed and drained spinach to the skillet. Season with salt and pepper. Cook for another 2-3 minutes until the spinach is heated through.

4. In a bowl, combine the cooked spinach mixture, crumbled feta cheese, ricotta cheese, and grated Parmesan cheese. Mix well.

5. Lay one sheet of phyllo dough on a clean surface and brush it lightly with melted butter.

6. Place another sheet of phyllo dough on top and brush it with butter. Repeat this process until you have a stack of 4-5 phyllo sheets.

7. Cut the phyllo stack into 3-inch wide strips.

8. Spoon a small amount of the spinach and cheese mixture onto one end of each strip.

9. Fold the corner of the phyllo strip over the filling to form a triangle, then continue folding diagonally until you reach the end of the strip. Seal the end with a little melted butter.

10. Place the filled phyllo triangles on the prepared baking sheet.

11. Brush the tops of the triangles with more melted butter.

12. Bake in the preheated oven for 20-25 minutes or until the phyllo is golden brown and crispy.

13. Remove from the oven and let the Spinach and Cheese Phyllo Triangles cool slightly before serving.

Eggplant Caviar (Ikra)

Servings: 6 Time: 1 hour

Ingredients:

- 2 large eggplants
- 2 tomatoes, diced
- 1 onion, finely chopped
- 2 cloves garlic, minced
- 2 tablespoons olive oil
- 1 tablespoon tomato paste
- Salt and pepper to taste
- Fresh parsley, chopped (for garnish)
- Toasted bread or crackers (for serving)

Directions:

1. Preheat your oven to 400°F (200°C). Pierce the eggplants with a fork and place them on a baking sheet. Roast in the oven for 30-40 minutes until the eggplants are tender and the skin is charred.

2. Remove the eggplants from the oven and let them cool. Peel off the charred skin and discard.

3. In a skillet, heat olive oil over medium heat. Add the chopped onion and minced garlic. Cook until the onion is soft and translucent, about 5 minutes.

4. Add the diced tomatoes and tomato paste to the skillet. Cook for another 5 minutes until the tomatoes soften and the mixture thickens.

5. Scoop out the flesh from the roasted eggplants and add it to the skillet. Mash the eggplant flesh with a fork and mix well with the tomato mixture.

6. Season with salt and pepper to taste. Cook for another 5-10 minutes until the flavors meld together.

7. Remove the Eggplant Caviar from heat and let it cool slightly.

8. Transfer the Eggplant Caviar to a serving dish, garnish with chopped parsley, and serve with toasted bread or crackers.

Herb Salad

Servings: 4 Time: 15 minutes

Ingredients:

- 2 cups mixed fresh herbs (such as parsley, cilantro, mint, and dill), chopped
- 1 cup cherry tomatoes, halved
- 1 cucumber, diced
- 1/4 red onion, thinly sliced
- Juice of 1 lemon
- 2 tablespoons olive oil
- Salt and pepper to taste

Directions:

1. In a large bowl, combine the chopped fresh herbs, halved cherry tomatoes, diced cucumber, and thinly sliced red onion.
2. Drizzle the lemon juice and olive oil over the salad ingredients.
3. Season with salt and pepper to taste.
4. Toss the salad gently to coat all the ingredients with the dressing.

Yogurt and Cucumber Dip (Tzatziki)

Servings: 4 Time: 15 minutes

Ingredients:

- 1 cup Greek yogurt
- 1 cucumber, grated and excess moisture squeezed out
- 2 cloves garlic, minced
- 1 tablespoon olive oil
- 1 tablespoon fresh dill, chopped
- 1 tablespoon fresh mint, chopped
- 1 tablespoon lemon juice
- Salt and pepper to taste

Directions:

1. In a mixing bowl, combine the Greek yogurt, grated cucumber, minced garlic, olive oil, chopped fresh dill, chopped fresh mint, and lemon juice.
2. Mix well to combine all the ingredients.
3. Season the Tzatziki dip with salt and pepper to taste.
4. Chill the dip in the refrigerator for at least 30 minutes to allow the flavors to meld together.
5. Before serving, give the Tzatziki dip a final stir and adjust the seasoning if needed.

6. Serve the chilled Yogurt and Cucumber Dip with pita bread, chips, or as a refreshing sauce for grilled meats or vegetables.

Cheese and Herb Stuffed Mushrooms

Servings: 4 Time: 30 minutes

Ingredients:

- 12 large mushrooms, stems removed and reserved
- 1/2 cup cream cheese, softened
- 1/4 cup grated Parmesan cheese
- 1/4 cup breadcrumbs
- 2 tablespoons chopped fresh parsley
- 1 tablespoon chopped fresh chives
- 1 tablespoon olive oil
- Salt and pepper to taste

Directions:

1. Preheat your oven to 375°F (190°C) and grease a baking dish.
2. Finely chop the reserved mushroom stems.
3. In a skillet, heat olive oil over medium heat. Add the chopped mushroom stems and cook until they are softened, about 5 minutes. Remove from heat and let them cool slightly.
4. In a mixing bowl, combine the softened cream cheese, grated Parmesan cheese, breadcrumbs, chopped parsley,

chopped chives, and cooked mushroom stems. Mix well to form a creamy filling. Season with salt and pepper to taste.

5. Spoon the cheese and herb filling into the hollowed-out mushroom caps, pressing gently to fill them evenly.

6. Place the stuffed mushrooms in the greased baking dish.

7. Bake in the preheated oven for 15-20 minutes or until the mushrooms are tender and the filling is golden and bubbly.

8. Remove from the oven and let the Cheese and Herb Stuffed Mushrooms cool slightly before serving.

Red Pepper and Walnut Spread (Muhammara)

Servings: 6 Time: 30 minutes

Ingredients:

- 2 large red bell peppers, roasted and peeled
- 1 cup walnuts, toasted
- 2 cloves garlic, minced
- 1 tablespoon tomato paste
- 1 tablespoon pomegranate molasses
- 1 teaspoon ground cumin
- 1/2 teaspoon smoked paprika
- 1/4 teaspoon cayenne pepper (optional, for heat)
- Salt and pepper to taste
- 2 tablespoons olive oil
- 1 tablespoon lemon juice
- Chopped fresh parsley or mint (for garnish)

Directions:

1. Roast the red bell peppers over an open flame or in the oven until the skin is charred. Place them in a bowl, cover with plastic wrap, and let them steam for about 10

minutes. Peel off the charred skin, remove the seeds and membranes, and chop the roasted peppers.

2. In a food processor, combine the toasted walnuts, minced garlic, chopped roasted peppers, tomato paste, pomegranate molasses, ground cumin, smoked paprika, cayenne pepper (if using), salt, and pepper.

3. Pulse the ingredients until they are finely chopped and well combined, but not completely smooth. You want some texture to remain.

4. With the food processor running, gradually drizzle in the olive oil and lemon juice until the mixture becomes a thick and creamy spread.

5. Taste the Muhammara and adjust the seasoning if needed, adding more salt, pepper, or lemon juice according to your preference.

6. Transfer the Muhammara to a serving bowl, drizzle with a little extra olive oil, and garnish with chopped fresh parsley or mint.

7. Serve the Red Pepper and Walnut Spread with pita bread, crackers, or as a flavorful dip for vegetables.

SOUPS AND SALADS

Lentil Soup

Servings: 6 Time: 1 hour

Ingredients:

- 1 cup dried green or brown lentils, rinsed and drained
- 1 onion, chopped
- 2 carrots, chopped
- 2 celery stalks, chopped
- 3 cloves garlic, minced
- 1 can (14 oz) diced tomatoes
- 6 cups vegetable or chicken broth
- 1 teaspoon ground cumin
- 1 teaspoon ground coriander

- 1/2 teaspoon turmeric powder
- Salt and pepper to taste
- 2 tablespoons olive oil
- Fresh parsley or cilantro, chopped (for garnish)
- Lemon wedges (optional, for serving)

Directions:

1. In a large pot, heat the olive oil over medium heat. Add the chopped onion, carrots, celery, and garlic. Cook until the vegetables are softened, about 5-7 minutes.
2. Add the rinsed lentils, diced tomatoes (with their juices), vegetable or chicken broth, ground cumin, ground coriander, turmeric powder, salt, and pepper to the pot. Stir well to combine.
3. Bring the soup to a boil, then reduce heat to low and simmer, covered, for about 30-40 minutes or until the lentils are tender.
4. Use an immersion blender to partially blend the soup to your desired consistency. You can leave it chunky or blend it until smooth.
5. Taste the soup and adjust the seasoning if needed, adding more salt and pepper if desired.

6. Ladle the Lentil Soup into bowls, garnish with chopped fresh parsley or cilantro, and serve with lemon wedges on the side for squeezing over the soup, if desired.

Tabbouleh Salad

Servings: 4 Time: 30 minutes

Ingredients:

- 1 cup bulgur wheat
- 1 1/2 cups boiling water
- 2 cups chopped fresh parsley
- 1/2 cup chopped fresh mint
- 2 tomatoes, diced
- 1 cucumber, diced
- 1/4 red onion, finely chopped
- Juice of 2 lemons
- 3 tablespoons olive oil
- Salt and pepper to taste

Directions:

1. Place the bulgur wheat in a heatproof bowl and pour the boiling water over it. Cover the bowl with a lid or plate and let it sit for about 20-30 minutes or until the bulgur is tender and has absorbed the water. Fluff the bulgur with a fork.

2. In a large mixing bowl, combine the cooked bulgur wheat, chopped fresh parsley, chopped fresh mint, diced tomatoes, diced cucumber, and finely chopped red onion.

3. In a small bowl, whisk together the lemon juice, olive oil, salt, and pepper to make the dressing.

4. Pour the dressing over the salad ingredients in the large mixing bowl.

5. Toss the Tabbouleh Salad gently to coat all the ingredients with the dressing.

6. Taste the salad and adjust the seasoning if needed, adding more salt, pepper, or lemon juice according to your preference.

7. Chill the Tabbouleh Salad in the refrigerator for at least 30 minutes before serving to allow the flavors to meld together.

Cucumber and Tomato Salad

Servings: 4 Time: 15 minutes

Ingredients:

- 2 cucumbers, diced
- 2 tomatoes, diced
- 1/4 red onion, thinly sliced
- 1/4 cup chopped fresh parsley
- 2 tablespoons chopped fresh mint
- Juice of 1 lemon
- 2 tablespoons olive oil
- Salt and pepper to taste

Directions:

1. In a large bowl, combine the diced cucumbers, diced tomatoes, thinly sliced red onion, chopped fresh parsley, and chopped fresh mint.
2. In a small bowl, whisk together the lemon juice, olive oil, salt, and pepper to make the dressing.
3. Pour the dressing over the salad ingredients in the large bowl.
4. Toss the Cucumber and Tomato Salad gently to coat all the ingredients with the dressing.

5. Taste the salad and adjust the seasoning if needed, adding more salt, pepper, or lemon juice according to your preference.

Yogurt Soup (Madzoonov Khorovats)

Servings: 4 Time: 30 minutes

Ingredients:

- 4 cups plain yogurt
- 4 cups water or vegetable broth
- 1/2 cup fine bulgur
- 1 onion, finely chopped
- 2 tablespoons butter or olive oil
- 2 tablespoons all-purpose flour
- 2 eggs, beaten
- 1/2 cup fresh mint, chopped
- Salt and pepper to taste
- Optional: red pepper flakes or paprika for garnish

Directions:

1. In a large pot, combine the plain yogurt and water (or vegetable broth) over medium heat. Stir well to combine.
2. Add the fine bulgur to the pot and stir. Let the mixture simmer gently while you prepare the rest of the ingredients.

3. In a skillet, heat the butter or olive oil over medium heat. Add the finely chopped onion and sauté until translucent, about 5 minutes.

4. Sprinkle the flour over the sautéed onions and stir to combine. Cook for another 2-3 minutes to remove the raw flour taste.

5. Gradually add a ladleful of the hot yogurt mixture from the pot into the skillet with the onion and flour mixture. Stir constantly to prevent lumps from forming.

6. Once the mixture in the skillet is smooth and slightly thickened, pour it back into the pot with the rest of the yogurt mixture. Stir well to combine.

7. Slowly pour the beaten eggs into the hot soup while stirring constantly. This will create ribbons of egg throughout the soup.

8. Add the chopped fresh mint to the soup and season with salt and pepper to taste. Stir well.

9. Continue to simmer the Yogurt Soup for another 5-10 minutes until the bulgur is cooked through and the flavors are well blended.

10. Remove the soup from heat and ladle into serving bowls.

11. Optionally, sprinkle with red pepper flakes or paprika for added flavor and garnish.

Beetroot Salad

Servings: 4 Time: 45 minutes

Ingredients:

- 4 medium-sized beetroots, cooked and peeled
- 1/2 cup Greek yogurt
- 2 tablespoons mayonnaise
- 1 tablespoon Dijon mustard
- 1 tablespoon honey
- 1 tablespoon apple cider vinegar
- Salt and pepper to taste
- 1/4 cup chopped fresh dill
- 1/4 cup chopped walnuts (optional, for garnish)

Directions:

1. Slice the cooked and peeled beetroots into thin rounds or cubes, according to your preference.
2. In a mixing bowl, combine the Greek yogurt, mayonnaise, Dijon mustard, honey, apple cider vinegar, salt, and pepper. Whisk until smooth and well combined.
3. Add the sliced beetroots to the dressing in the bowl. Gently toss to coat the beetroots evenly with the dressing.

4. Sprinkle the chopped fresh dill over the Beetroot Salad and toss again to distribute the dill throughout the salad.

5. Optionally, garnish the salad with chopped walnuts for added texture and flavor.

6. Chill the Beetroot Salad in the refrigerator for at least 30 minutes before serving to allow the flavors to meld together.

Green Lentil Salad with Herbs

Servings: 4 Time: 30 minutes

Ingredients:

- 1 cup green lentils
- 2 cups water
- 1/2 red onion, finely chopped
- 1/2 cucumber, diced
- 1/2 red bell pepper, diced
- 1/4 cup chopped fresh parsley
- 1/4 cup chopped fresh mint
- 2 tablespoons olive oil
- Juice of 1 lemon
- Salt and pepper to taste

Directions:

1. Rinse the green lentils under cold water and drain.
2. In a saucepan, combine the rinsed lentils and water. Bring to a boil, then reduce heat to low and simmer, covered, for about 20-25 minutes or until the lentils are tender but still hold their shape. Drain any excess water and let the lentils cool.

3. In a large mixing bowl, combine the cooked and cooled lentils, finely chopped red onion, diced cucumber, diced red bell pepper, chopped fresh parsley, and chopped fresh mint.

4. In a small bowl, whisk together the olive oil, lemon juice, salt, and pepper to make the dressing.

5. Pour the dressing over the lentil and herb mixture in the large bowl.

6. Toss the Green Lentil Salad gently to coat all the ingredients with the dressing.

7. Taste the salad and adjust the seasoning if needed, adding more salt, pepper, or lemon juice according to your preference.

8. Chill the Green Lentil Salad in the refrigerator for at least 30 minutes before serving to allow the flavors to meld together.

Cold Cucumber Soup (Tzvika)

Servings: 4 Time: 20 minutes, plus chilling time

Ingredients:

- 2 cucumbers, peeled and grated
- 2 cups plain yogurt
- 1 cup cold water
- 2 tablespoons fresh dill, chopped
- 2 tablespoons fresh mint, chopped
- 1 clove garlic, minced
- 1 tablespoon olive oil
- Juice of 1 lemon
- Salt and pepper to taste
- Ice cubes (optional, for serving)

Directions:

1. In a large bowl, combine the grated cucumbers, plain yogurt, cold water, chopped fresh dill, chopped fresh mint, minced garlic, olive oil, and lemon juice.
2. Stir the ingredients until well combined.
3. Season the Cold Cucumber Soup (Tzvika) with salt and pepper to taste. Adjust the seasoning if needed.

4. Cover the bowl and refrigerate the soup for at least 2 hours to chill and allow the flavors to blend.

5. Before serving, give the soup a stir. If desired, add ice cubes to each serving bowl to keep the soup extra cold.

Potato Salad

Servings: 6 Time: 30 minutes

Ingredients:

- 2 lbs (about 1 kg) potatoes, peeled and diced into cubes
- 1/2 cup mayonnaise
- 2 tablespoons Dijon mustard
- 1 tablespoon apple cider vinegar
- 1/4 cup chopped red onion
- 1/4 cup chopped celery
- 1/4 cup chopped dill pickles
- 2 hard-boiled eggs, chopped
- Salt and pepper to taste
- Paprika for garnish (optional)

Directions:

1. Place the diced potatoes in a pot of salted water. Bring to a boil and cook until the potatoes are fork-tender but still firm, about 10-15 minutes. Drain and let them cool slightly.

2. In a large mixing bowl, combine the mayonnaise, Dijon mustard, apple cider vinegar, chopped red onion,

chopped celery, and chopped dill pickles. Mix well to make the dressing.

3. Add the cooked and slightly cooled potatoes to the dressing in the bowl.

4. Add the chopped hard-boiled eggs to the bowl.

5. Gently toss all the ingredients together until the potatoes and eggs are coated evenly with the dressing.

6. Season the Potato Salad with salt and pepper to taste. Adjust the seasoning if needed.

7. Cover the bowl and refrigerate the Potato Salad for at least 1 hour before serving to chill and allow the flavors to meld.

8. Before serving, give the Potato Salad a final stir. Optionally, sprinkle paprika over the top for garnish.

9. Serve the Potato Salad cold as a delicious side dish or part of a picnic or barbecue spread.

Mixed Bean Salad

Servings: 6 Time: 15 minutes

Ingredients:

- 1 can (15 oz) mixed beans (such as kidney beans, black beans, chickpeas), drained and rinsed
- 1 cup cherry tomatoes, halved
- 1/2 cucumber, diced
- 1/4 red onion, finely chopped
- 1/4 cup chopped fresh parsley
- 2 tablespoons olive oil
- 2 tablespoons balsamic vinegar
- 1 teaspoon Dijon mustard
- Salt and pepper to taste
- Crumbled feta cheese (optional, for garnish)

Directions:

1. In a large mixing bowl, combine the drained and rinsed mixed beans, halved cherry tomatoes, diced cucumber, finely chopped red onion, and chopped fresh parsley.
2. In a small bowl, whisk together the olive oil, balsamic vinegar, Dijon mustard, salt, and pepper to make the dressing.

3. Pour the dressing over the mixed bean salad ingredients in the large bowl.

4. Toss the salad gently to coat all the ingredients with the dressing.

5. Taste the Mixed Bean Salad and adjust the seasoning if needed, adding more salt, pepper, or vinegar according to your preference.

6. Optionally, sprinkle crumbled feta cheese over the top of the salad for added flavor and garnish.

Chickpea Soup (Shorabat Adas)

Servings: 4 Time: 1 hour

Ingredients:

- 1 cup dried chickpeas, soaked overnight and drained
- 1 onion, chopped
- 2 carrots, chopped
- 2 celery stalks, chopped
- 3 cloves garlic, minced
- 6 cups vegetable or chicken broth
- 1 teaspoon ground cumin
- 1 teaspoon ground coriander
- 1/2 teaspoon turmeric powder
- 1/2 teaspoon paprika
- Salt and pepper to taste
- 2 tablespoons olive oil
- Juice of 1 lemon
- Fresh parsley, chopped (for garnish)

Directions:

1. In a large pot, heat the olive oil over medium heat. Add the chopped onion, carrots, celery, and garlic. Cook until the vegetables are softened, about 5-7 minutes.

2. Add the soaked and drained chickpeas to the pot. Stir well to combine with the vegetables.

3. Pour in the vegetable or chicken broth. Add the ground cumin, ground coriander, turmeric powder, paprika, salt, and pepper. Stir to combine all the ingredients.

4. Bring the soup to a boil, then reduce heat to low and simmer, covered, for about 40-45 minutes or until the chickpeas are tender.

5. Use an immersion blender to partially blend the soup to your desired consistency. You can leave it chunky or blend it until smooth.

6. Squeeze in the juice of one lemon and stir well.

7. Taste the Chickpea Soup (Shorabat Adas) and adjust the seasoning if needed, adding more salt, pepper, or lemon juice according to your preference.

8. Ladle the soup into serving bowls, garnish with chopped fresh parsley, and serve hot.

MAIN COURSES

Stuffed Bell Peppers

Servings: 4 Time: 1 hour

Ingredients:

- 4 large bell peppers (any color), tops cut off and seeds removed
- 1 cup cooked rice (white or brown)
- 1 lb ground beef or turkey
- 1 onion, finely chopped
- 2 cloves garlic, minced
- 1 can (14 oz) diced tomatoes, drained
- 1 cup shredded cheese (such as cheddar or mozzarella), divided

- 1 teaspoon dried oregano
- 1 teaspoon dried basil
- Salt and pepper to taste
- Olive oil for cooking

Directions:

1. Preheat your oven to 375°F (190°C).
2. In a skillet, heat some olive oil over medium heat. Add the chopped onion and minced garlic. Cook until the onion is translucent, about 5 minutes.
3. Add the ground beef or turkey to the skillet. Cook until browned and cooked through, breaking it up with a spoon as it cooks.
4. Stir in the cooked rice, diced tomatoes (drained), dried oregano, dried basil, salt, and pepper. Cook for another 2-3 minutes until well combined and heated through.
5. Remove the skillet from heat and stir in half of the shredded cheese.
6. Stuff each bell pepper with the meat and rice mixture, packing it tightly.
7. Place the stuffed bell peppers upright in a baking dish. Drizzle a little olive oil over the tops of the peppers.
8. Cover the baking dish with aluminum foil and bake in the preheated oven for 30 minutes.

9. After 30 minutes, remove the foil and sprinkle the remaining shredded cheese over the tops of the peppers.

10. Bake, uncovered, for another 10-15 minutes or until the cheese is melted and bubbly, and the peppers are tender.

11. Remove from the oven and let the Stuffed Bell Peppers cool slightly before serving.

Grilled Lamb Kebabs (Shish Kebab)

Servings: 4 Time: 1 hour (including marinating time)

Ingredients:

- 1 lb lamb meat (leg or shoulder), cut into 1-inch cubes
- 1 onion, grated
- 2 cloves garlic, minced
- 2 tablespoons olive oil
- Juice of 1 lemon
- 1 teaspoon paprika
- 1 teaspoon ground cumin
- 1 teaspoon ground coriander
- Salt and pepper to taste
- Skewers (metal or soaked wooden skewers)

Directions:

1. In a bowl, combine the grated onion, minced garlic, olive oil, lemon juice, paprika, ground cumin, ground coriander, salt, and pepper to make the marinade.

2. Add the lamb cubes to the marinade and toss to coat the meat evenly. Cover the bowl and refrigerate for at least 30 minutes to marinate, or longer for more flavor (up to overnight).

3. Preheat your grill to medium-high heat.

4. Thread the marinated lamb cubes onto skewers, leaving a little space between each piece.

5. Grill the lamb kebabs over medium-high heat, turning occasionally, for about 10-12 minutes or until the meat is cooked to your desired doneness and has nice grill marks.

6. Remove the grilled Lamb Kebabs from the grill and let them rest for a few minutes before serving.

7. Serve the Grilled Lamb Kebabs hot with your choice of sides, such as rice, salad, or grilled vegetables.

Chicken Pilaf

Servings: 4 Time: 45 minutes

Ingredients:

- 1 cup long-grain white rice
- 1 lb boneless, skinless chicken breasts or thighs, cut into bite-sized pieces
- 1 onion, chopped
- 2 cloves garlic, minced
- 2 carrots, diced
- 1 red bell pepper, diced
- 1 teaspoon ground cumin
- 1 teaspoon ground coriander
- 1 teaspoon turmeric powder
- Salt and pepper to taste
- 2 cups chicken broth
- 2 tablespoons olive oil or butter
- Fresh parsley or cilantro, chopped (for garnish)
- Lemon wedges (optional, for serving)

Directions:

1. Rinse the rice under cold water until the water runs clear. Drain and set aside.

2. In a large skillet or pot, heat the olive oil or butter over medium heat. Add the chopped onion and minced garlic. Cook until the onion is translucent, about 5 minutes.

3. Add the diced chicken to the skillet. Cook until the chicken is browned on all sides, about 5-7 minutes.

4. Stir in the diced carrots and red bell pepper. Cook for another 3-4 minutes until the vegetables begin to soften.

5. Add the ground cumin, ground coriander, turmeric powder, salt, and pepper to the skillet. Stir well to coat the chicken and vegetables with the spices.

6. Pour in the chicken broth and bring the mixture to a boil.

7. Add the rinsed and drained rice to the skillet. Stir to combine with the chicken and vegetables.

8. Reduce heat to low, cover the skillet with a lid, and simmer for about 15-20 minutes or until the rice is tender and has absorbed the liquid.

9. Remove the Chicken Pilaf from heat and let it rest, covered, for a few minutes.

10. Fluff the pilaf with a fork to mix the chicken, vegetables, and rice evenly.

11. Serve the Chicken Pilaf hot, garnished with chopped fresh parsley or cilantro. Offer lemon wedges on the side for squeezing over the pilaf, if desired.

Vegetable Moussaka

Servings: 6-8 Time: 1 hour 30 minutes

Ingredients:

- 2 large eggplants, sliced lengthwise into 1/4-inch thick slices
- Salt
- Olive oil for brushing
- 1 lb potatoes, peeled and thinly sliced
- 1 onion, chopped
- 2 cloves garlic, minced
- 1 red bell pepper, chopped
- 1 zucchini, diced
- 1 carrot, diced
- 1 can (14 oz) diced tomatoes, drained
- 1 teaspoon dried oregano
- 1 teaspoon dried thyme
- Salt and pepper to taste
- 1/2 cup grated Parmesan cheese
- 1/2 cup breadcrumbs

For the Bechamel Sauce:

- 4 tablespoons butter

- 1/4 cup all-purpose flour
- 2 cups milk
- Salt and pepper to taste
- Pinch of nutmeg
- 2 eggs, beaten

Directions:

1. Preheat your oven to 400°F (200°C).
2. Place the eggplant slices in a colander and sprinkle them with salt. Let them sit for about 30 minutes to release excess moisture. Rinse the eggplant slices and pat them dry with paper towels.
3. Brush the eggplant slices with olive oil and place them on a baking sheet. Roast in the preheated oven for about 15-20 minutes or until tender. Remove from the oven and set aside.
4. In a large skillet, heat some olive oil over medium heat. Add the chopped onion and minced garlic. Cook until the onion is translucent, about 5 minutes.
5. Add the chopped red bell pepper, diced zucchini, and diced carrot to the skillet. Cook for another 5 minutes until the vegetables are slightly softened.
6. Stir in the drained diced tomatoes, dried oregano, dried thyme, salt, and pepper. Cook for a few more minutes

until the flavors meld together. Remove from heat and set aside.

7. In a separate saucepan, melt the butter over medium heat for the bechamel sauce. Add the flour and whisk continuously until the mixture is smooth and bubbly, about 2 minutes.

8. Gradually pour in the milk, whisking constantly to avoid lumps. Cook the sauce until it thickens, about 5-7 minutes.

9. Season the bechamel sauce with salt, pepper, and a pinch of nutmeg. Remove from heat.

10. Gradually whisk the beaten eggs into the sauce until well combined.

11. To assemble the moussaka, layer half of the roasted eggplant slices in the bottom of a greased baking dish. Top with half of the cooked vegetable mixture.

12. Arrange the thinly sliced potatoes over the vegetables in the baking dish.

13. Sprinkle half of the grated Parmesan cheese over the potato layer.

14. Repeat the layers with the remaining eggplant slices, vegetables, and Parmesan cheese.

15. Pour the prepared bechamel sauce evenly over the top layer of the moussaka.

16. Sprinkle breadcrumbs over the top of the moussaka.

17. Cover the baking dish with foil and bake in the preheated oven for about 30-40 minutes.

18. Remove the foil and bake for an additional 10-15 minutes or until the top is golden brown and bubbly.

19. Remove the Vegetable Moussaka from the oven and let it cool slightly before serving.

Beef Kofta

Servings: 4 Time: 30 minutes

Ingredients:

- 1 lb ground beef (lean)
- 1 onion, grated
- 2 cloves garlic, minced
- 1/4 cup fresh parsley, chopped
- 1/4 cup fresh cilantro, chopped
- 1 teaspoon ground cumin
- 1 teaspoon ground coriander
- 1/2 teaspoon paprika
- Salt and pepper to taste
- Olive oil for cooking
- Skewers (metal or soaked wooden skewers)

Directions:

1. Preheat your grill or grill pan over medium-high heat.
2. In a large mixing bowl, combine the ground beef, grated onion, minced garlic, chopped fresh parsley, chopped fresh cilantro, ground cumin, ground coriander, paprika, salt, and pepper. Mix well until all ingredients are evenly incorporated.

3. Take a portion of the meat mixture and shape it into a sausage-like cylinder around a skewer. Press and mold the meat firmly to secure it on the skewer. Repeat with the remaining meat mixture.

4. Brush the beef kofta skewers with olive oil to prevent sticking.

5. Place the skewers on the preheated grill or grill pan. Cook for about 5-7 minutes on each side, or until the kofta is cooked through and has nice grill marks.

6. Remove the Beef Kofta skewers from the grill and let them rest for a few minutes before serving.

7. Serve the Beef Kofta hot with your choice of sides, such as rice, salad, or grilled vegetables.

Stuffed Zucchini (Kousa Mahshi)

Servings: 4 Time: 1 hour 15 minutes

Ingredients:

- 4 medium zucchini
- 1 cup rice, rinsed and drained
- 1/2 lb ground beef or lamb
- 1 onion, finely chopped
- 2 tomatoes, finely chopped
- 2 tablespoons tomato paste
- 2 tablespoons olive oil
- 1/4 cup chopped fresh parsley
- 1/4 cup chopped fresh mint
- 1 teaspoon ground cinnamon
- Salt and pepper to taste
- Water or broth for cooking

Directions:

1. Preheat your oven to 375°F (190°C).
2. Cut the tops off the zucchini and hollow them out using a spoon, leaving about a 1/4-inch thick shell. Reserve the scooped-out flesh.

3. In a bowl, combine the rinsed rice, ground beef or lamb, finely chopped onion, finely chopped tomatoes, tomato paste, olive oil, chopped fresh parsley, chopped fresh mint, ground cinnamon, salt, and pepper. Mix well to combine.

4. Stuff the hollowed zucchini with the rice and meat mixture, packing it tightly.

5. Place the stuffed zucchini in a baking dish. Arrange them snugly to prevent them from tipping over during baking.

6. Chop the reserved zucchini flesh and scatter it around the stuffed zucchini in the baking dish.

7. Pour enough water or broth into the baking dish to cover the bottom.

8. Cover the baking dish with aluminum foil and bake in the preheated oven for about 45-50 minutes or until the zucchini and rice are tender.

9. Remove the foil and bake for another 10-15 minutes or until the tops of the stuffed zucchini are lightly browned.

10. Remove the Stuffed Zucchini (Kousa Mahshi) from the oven and let them cool slightly before serving.

Lamb Stew (Khashlama)

Servings: 4 Time: 2 hours

Ingredients:

- 1 lb lamb stew meat, cut into bite-sized pieces
- 2 onions, sliced
- 3 carrots, peeled and sliced
- 2 potatoes, peeled and cubed
- 1 bell pepper, sliced
- 2 tomatoes, chopped
- 4 cloves garlic, minced
- 1 teaspoon paprika
- 1 teaspoon ground cumin
- 1 teaspoon dried thyme
- Salt and pepper to taste
- 2 cups beef or vegetable broth
- 2 tablespoons olive oil
- Fresh parsley or cilantro, chopped (for garnish)

Directions:

1. In a large pot or Dutch oven, heat the olive oil over medium heat. Add the sliced onions and minced garlic. Cook until the onions are translucent, about 5 minutes.

2. Add the lamb stew meat to the pot. Cook until the meat is browned on all sides, about 8-10 minutes.

3. Stir in the sliced carrots, cubed potatoes, sliced bell pepper, chopped tomatoes, paprika, ground cumin, dried thyme, salt, and pepper. Mix well to combine.

4. Pour in the beef or vegetable broth to cover the ingredients in the pot.

5. Bring the stew to a boil, then reduce heat to low. Cover the pot and simmer for about 1.5 to 2 hours, or until the lamb is tender and the vegetables are cooked through.

6. Check the seasoning of the Lamb Stew (Khashlama) and adjust salt and pepper if needed.

7. Remove the stew from heat and let it rest for a few minutes.

8. Serve the Lamb Stew hot, garnished with chopped fresh parsley or cilantro.

Eggplant and Chickpea Casserole

Servings: 4-6 Time: 1 hour

Ingredients:

- 2 large eggplants, sliced into rounds
- Salt
- Olive oil for brushing
- 1 can (15 oz) chickpeas, drained and rinsed
- 1 onion, chopped
- 3 cloves garlic, minced
- 1 bell pepper, chopped
- 1 can (14 oz) diced tomatoes, drained
- 1 teaspoon dried oregano
- 1 teaspoon dried basil
- Salt and pepper to taste
- 1 cup shredded mozzarella cheese
- Fresh basil leaves, chopped (for garnish)

Directions:

1. Preheat your oven to 400°F (200°C).
2. Place the eggplant slices in a colander and sprinkle them with salt. Let them sit for about 30 minutes to release

excess moisture. Rinse the eggplant slices and pat them dry with paper towels.

3. Brush the eggplant slices with olive oil and place them on a baking sheet. Roast in the preheated oven for about 15-20 minutes or until tender. Remove from the oven and set aside.

4. In a skillet, heat some olive oil over medium heat. Add the chopped onion and minced garlic. Cook until the onion is translucent, about 5 minutes.

5. Add the chopped bell pepper to the skillet. Cook for another 3-4 minutes until the pepper is slightly softened.

6. Stir in the drained chickpeas, diced tomatoes (drained), dried oregano, dried basil, salt, and pepper. Cook for a few more minutes until the flavors meld together.

7. In a greased casserole dish, layer half of the roasted eggplant slices on the bottom.

8. Spread half of the chickpea and tomato mixture over the eggplant layer.

9. Sprinkle half of the shredded mozzarella cheese over the chickpea layer.

10. Repeat the layers with the remaining eggplant slices, chickpea and tomato mixture, and shredded mozzarella cheese.

11. Cover the casserole dish with foil and bake in the preheated oven for about 20-25 minutes.

12. Remove the foil and bake for another 10 minutes or until the cheese is melted and bubbly.

13. Remove the Eggplant and Chickpea Casserole from the oven and let it cool slightly before serving.

14. Garnish with chopped fresh basil leaves before serving.

TRADITIONAL ARMENIAN COOKBOOK

Fish Kebabs

Servings: 4 Time: 30 minutes

Ingredients:

- 1 lb firm fish fillets (such as cod, halibut, or salmon), cut into 1-inch cubes
- 1 onion, finely chopped
- 2 cloves garlic, minced
- 1/4 cup fresh parsley, chopped
- 1/4 cup fresh cilantro, chopped
- Juice of 1 lemon
- 2 tablespoons olive oil
- 1 teaspoon ground cumin
- 1 teaspoon paprika
- Salt and pepper to taste
- Skewers (metal or soaked wooden skewers)

Directions:

1. In a bowl, combine the finely chopped onion, minced garlic, chopped fresh parsley, chopped fresh cilantro, lemon juice, olive oil, ground cumin, paprika, salt, and pepper. Mix well to make the marinade.

2. Add the fish cubes to the marinade and toss gently to coat. Cover the bowl and refrigerate for at least 20-30 minutes to marinate.

3. Preheat your grill or grill pan over medium-high heat.

4. Thread the marinated fish cubes onto skewers, leaving a little space between each piece.

5. Brush the fish kebabs with a little olive oil to prevent sticking.

6. Grill the fish kebabs on the preheated grill or grill pan for about 3-4 minutes on each side, or until the fish is cooked through and has grill marks.

7. Remove the Fish Kebabs from the grill and let them rest for a few minutes before serving.

8. Serve the Fish Kebabs hot with a side of lemon wedges and your choice of salad or grilled vegetables.

Lentil and Rice Pilaf (Mjaddara)

Servings: 4-6 Time: 40 minutes

Ingredients:

- 1 cup brown or green lentils, rinsed
- 1 cup long-grain white rice
- 1 onion, thinly sliced
- 2 tablespoons olive oil
- 1 teaspoon ground cumin
- 1 teaspoon ground coriander
- 1/2 teaspoon ground cinnamon
- Salt and pepper to taste
- 2 cups vegetable or chicken broth
- Fresh parsley or cilantro, chopped (for garnish)

Directions:

1. In a large pot, heat the olive oil over medium heat. Add the thinly sliced onion and cook until golden and caramelized, about 10-15 minutes. Remove half of the caramelized onions and set aside for garnish.
2. To the pot with the remaining caramelized onions, add the ground cumin, ground coriander, ground cinnamon,

salt, and pepper. Stir to combine and cook for another minute.

3. Add the rinsed lentils to the pot and stir to coat them with the onion and spice mixture.

4. Pour in the vegetable or chicken broth and bring the mixture to a boil.

5. Once boiling, reduce the heat to low, cover the pot with a lid, and simmer for about 15-20 minutes or until the lentils are tender.

6. Stir in the long-grain white rice into the pot with the lentils. If needed, add a little more broth or water to ensure there's enough liquid to cook the rice.

7. Cover the pot again and simmer for another 15-20 minutes, or until the rice is cooked and fluffy and has absorbed most of the liquid.

8. Remove the Lentil and Rice Pilaf (Mjaddara) from heat and let it rest, covered, for a few minutes.

9. Fluff the pilaf with a fork to mix the lentils and rice evenly.

10. Serve the Lentil and Rice Pilaf hot, garnished with the reserved caramelized onions and chopped fresh parsley or cilantro.

SIDE DISHES

Roasted Vegetables

Servings: 4 Time: 30 minutes

Ingredients:

- 1 lb mixed vegetables (such as carrots, bell peppers, zucchini, broccoli, cauliflower, etc.), cut into bite-sized pieces
- 2 tablespoons olive oil
- 1 teaspoon dried herbs (such as thyme, rosemary, or Italian seasoning)
- Salt and pepper to taste
- Optional: minced garlic, grated Parmesan cheese, balsamic vinegar

Directions:

1. Preheat your oven to 400°F (200°C).

2. In a large bowl, toss the mixed vegetables with olive oil, dried herbs, salt, and pepper until evenly coated.

3. Spread the vegetables in a single layer on a baking sheet lined with parchment paper or aluminum foil.

4. Roast the vegetables in the preheated oven for about 20-25 minutes, or until they are tender and slightly caramelized, stirring halfway through cooking.

5. Optional: If using minced garlic, sprinkle it over the vegetables during the last 5 minutes of roasting for added flavor.

6. Remove the Roasted Vegetables from the oven and transfer them to a serving dish.

7. If desired, sprinkle grated Parmesan cheese over the vegetables while they are still hot.

8. Drizzle with balsamic vinegar just before serving.

Green Bean Salad with Feta and Lemon Dressing:

Servings: 4 Time: 20 minutes

Ingredients:

- 1 pound fresh green beans, trimmed
- 1/2 cup crumbled feta cheese
- 1/4 cup chopped fresh parsley
- 1/4 cup chopped red onion
- Zest of 1 lemon
- 2 tablespoons lemon juice
- 2 tablespoons extra-virgin olive oil
- Salt and pepper to taste

Instructions:

1. Bring a pot of salted water to a boil. Add the green beans and cook for 3-4 minutes until tender-crisp. Drain and rinse under cold water to stop the cooking process. Pat dry with a paper towel.
2. In a large bowl, combine the cooked green beans, crumbled feta cheese, chopped parsley, and chopped red onion.

3. In a small bowl, whisk together the lemon zest, lemon juice, and extra-virgin olive oil to make the dressing. Season with salt and pepper to taste.

4. Pour the lemon dressing over the green bean mixture and toss gently to coat everything evenly.

Pickled Vegetables

Ingredients:

- 2 cups mixed vegetables (such as carrots, cucumbers, bell peppers, cauliflower, etc.), sliced or cut into bite-sized pieces
- 1 cup white vinegar
- 1 cup water
- 2 tablespoons sugar
- 1 tablespoon salt
- Optional: garlic cloves, whole peppercorns, dried herbs (such as dill, thyme, or bay leaves)

Instructions:

1. Prepare your vegetables by washing and slicing them into the desired size and shape. You can use a mix of vegetables or focus on one type, depending on your preference.
2. In a saucepan, combine the white vinegar, water, sugar, salt, and any optional spices or herbs you'd like to use. Bring the mixture to a boil, stirring until the sugar and salt dissolve completely.
3. Remove the brine mixture from heat and let it cool to room temperature.

4. Place the prepared vegetables in clean, sterilized glass jars. Add garlic cloves, whole peppercorns, and any other spices or herbs to the jars for extra flavor, if desired.

5. Pour the cooled brine over the vegetables in the jars, making sure they are completely submerged in the liquid.

6. Seal the jars tightly with lids and store them in the refrigerator for at least 24 hours before serving to allow the flavors to develop.

Bulgur Pilaf with Mushrooms

Servings: 4 Time: 30 minutes

Ingredients:

- 1 cup bulgur wheat
- 2 cups vegetable or chicken broth
- 1 onion, finely chopped
- 2 cloves garlic, minced
- 8 oz mushrooms, sliced
- 2 tablespoons olive oil
- Salt and pepper to taste
- Fresh parsley, chopped (for garnish)

Instructions:

1. Rinse the bulgur wheat under cold water and drain well.
2. In a saucepan, heat the olive oil over medium heat. Add the chopped onion and minced garlic. Cook until the onion is translucent, about 5 minutes.
3. Add the sliced mushrooms to the saucepan. Cook until the mushrooms are softened and golden brown, about 5-7 minutes.
4. Stir in the bulgur wheat and coat it with the onion and mushroom mixture.

5. Pour in the vegetable or chicken broth and bring the mixture to a boil.

6. Once boiling, reduce the heat to low, cover the saucepan with a lid, and simmer for about 15-20 minutes or until the bulgur is tender and has absorbed the liquid.

7. Fluff the Bulgur Pilaf with Mushrooms with a fork to mix the ingredients evenly.

8. Season with salt and pepper to taste.

9. Serve the pilaf hot, garnished with chopped fresh parsley.

Cabbage Rolls (Kalam Dolma)

Servings: 6-8 Time: 1 hour 30 minutes

Ingredients:

- 1 large head of cabbage
- 1 lb ground beef or lamb
- 1 onion, finely chopped
- 1/2 cup rice, rinsed
- 1 can (14 oz) diced tomatoes
- 2 tablespoons tomato paste
- 2 cloves garlic, minced
- 1 teaspoon dried mint
- 1 teaspoon dried dill
- Salt and pepper to taste
- 2 cups beef or vegetable broth
- 2 tablespoons olive oil
- Fresh parsley, chopped (for garnish)
- Lemon wedges (for serving)

Instructions:

1. Preheat your oven to 350°F (175°C).
2. Remove the core from the cabbage and place the whole cabbage in a large pot of boiling water. Cook for about 10

minutes or until the outer leaves are tender and can be easily separated. Remove the cabbage from the water and let it cool slightly.

3. In a bowl, mix together the ground beef or lamb, finely chopped onion, rinsed rice, minced garlic, dried mint, dried dill, salt, and pepper.

4. Carefully peel off the softened outer leaves of the cabbage and trim the thick stem at the base of each leaf.

5. Place a spoonful of the meat and rice mixture onto the center of each cabbage leaf. Roll the leaf tightly, tucking in the sides as you roll, to form a cabbage roll.

6. In a large oven-safe dish, spread a layer of diced tomatoes and tomato paste on the bottom.

7. Arrange the cabbage rolls seam-side down in the dish, making sure they are snugly packed together.

8. Pour the beef or vegetable broth over the cabbage rolls.

9. Drizzle the olive oil over the cabbage rolls and cover the dish with aluminum foil.

10. Bake in the preheated oven for about 45-50 minutes or until the cabbage rolls are cooked through and tender.

11. Remove the foil and bake for an additional 10-15 minutes to brown the tops slightly.

12. Remove the Cabbage Rolls (Kalam Dolma) from the oven and let them cool for a few minutes.

13. Serve the cabbage rolls hot, garnished with chopped fresh parsley and lemon wedges on the side.

Spinach and Cheese Stuffed Bell Peppers

Servings: 4 Time: 45 minutes

Ingredients:

- 4 large bell peppers (any color), tops cut off and seeds removed
- 1 tablespoon olive oil
- 1 onion, finely chopped
- 2 cloves garlic, minced
- 6 cups fresh spinach leaves, chopped
- 1 cup cooked quinoa or rice
- 1 cup shredded mozzarella cheese
- 1/4 cup grated Parmesan cheese
- Salt and pepper to taste
- Optional: red pepper flakes, chopped fresh herbs (such as parsley or basil)

Instructions:

1. Preheat your oven to 375°F (190°C).
2. Heat olive oil in a skillet over medium heat. Add the finely chopped onion and minced garlic. Cook until the onion is translucent, about 5 minutes.

3. Add the chopped fresh spinach to the skillet. Cook until the spinach is wilted and cooked down, about 3-4 minutes. Remove from heat.

4. In a large bowl, combine the cooked quinoa or rice, shredded mozzarella cheese, grated Parmesan cheese, and the cooked spinach mixture from the skillet. Season with salt and pepper to taste. Add red pepper flakes or chopped fresh herbs if desired.

5. Stuff the prepared bell peppers with the spinach and cheese mixture, packing it tightly and mounding it on top.

6. Place the stuffed bell peppers in a baking dish. If there's leftover filling, you can sprinkle it around the peppers in the dish.

7. Cover the baking dish with aluminum foil and bake in the preheated oven for about 25-30 minutes.

8. Remove the foil and bake for an additional 10-15 minutes or until the bell peppers are tender and the filling is heated through and lightly browned on top.

9. Remove the Spinach and Cheese Stuffed Bell Peppers from the oven and let them cool for a few minutes before serving.

Herb Pilaf

Servings: 4 Time: 30 minutes

Ingredients:

- 1 cup long-grain white rice
- 2 cups vegetable or chicken broth
- 2 tablespoons olive oil
- 1 onion, finely chopped
- 2 cloves garlic, minced
- 1/4 cup chopped fresh parsley
- 1/4 cup chopped fresh cilantro
- 1/4 cup chopped fresh dill
- Salt and pepper to taste
- Optional: lemon zest

Instructions:

1. Rinse the rice under cold water until the water runs clear. Drain well.
2. In a saucepan, heat the olive oil over medium heat. Add the finely chopped onion and minced garlic. Cook until the onion is translucent, about 5 minutes.
3. Add the rinsed rice to the saucepan. Stir to coat the rice with the onion and garlic mixture.

4. Pour in the vegetable or chicken broth and bring the mixture to a boil.

5. Once boiling, reduce the heat to low, cover the saucepan with a lid, and simmer for about 15-20 minutes or until the rice is tender and has absorbed the liquid.

6. Remove the saucepan from heat and let it sit, covered, for a few minutes.

7. Fluff the Herb Pilaf with a fork to mix the herbs evenly throughout the rice.

8. Season with salt and pepper to taste. If desired, add a sprinkle of lemon zest for a citrusy flavor.

Green Beans with Tomatoes

Servings: 4 Time: 25 minutes

Ingredients:

- 1 lb fresh green beans, trimmed and halved
- 2 tablespoons olive oil
- 1 onion, finely chopped
- 2 cloves garlic, minced
- 2 cups cherry tomatoes, halved
- Salt and pepper to taste
- Fresh basil leaves, chopped (for garnish)

Instructions:

1. Bring a pot of salted water to a boil. Add the trimmed and halved green beans to the boiling water and cook for about 3-4 minutes, or until they are crisp-tender. Drain the green beans and set aside.

2. In a large skillet, heat the olive oil over medium heat. Add the finely chopped onion and minced garlic. Cook until the onion is translucent and the garlic is fragrant, about 3-4 minutes.

3. Add the halved cherry tomatoes to the skillet. Cook for another 3-4 minutes, or until the tomatoes start to soften and release their juices.

4. Add the cooked green beans to the skillet with the tomatoes. Season with salt and pepper to taste. Stir to coat the green beans evenly with the tomato mixture.

5. Cook the green beans and tomatoes together for an additional 2-3 minutes, allowing the flavors to meld.

6. Remove the skillet from heat and transfer the Green Beans with Tomatoes to a serving dish.

7. Garnish with chopped fresh basil leaves before serving.

Potato Kebabs (Kartoflu Kebab)

Servings: 4-6 Time: 1 hour

Ingredients:

- 4 large potatoes, peeled and cubed
- 1 onion, finely chopped
- 2 cloves garlic, minced
- 1/2 cup breadcrumbs
- 1/4 cup grated Parmesan cheese
- 1/4 cup chopped fresh parsley
- 1 teaspoon dried oregano
- 1 teaspoon paprika
- Salt and pepper to taste
- Olive oil for frying

Instructions:

1. Boil the cubed potatoes in salted water until tender, about 10-15 minutes. Drain the potatoes and let them cool slightly.
2. In a large bowl, mash the boiled potatoes until smooth.
3. Add the finely chopped onion, minced garlic, breadcrumbs, grated Parmesan cheese, chopped fresh parsley, dried oregano, paprika, salt, and pepper to the

mashed potatoes. Mix well to combine all the ingredients.

4. Shape the potato mixture into small kebab shapes or patties.

5. Heat olive oil in a skillet over medium heat. Add the potato kebabs to the skillet in batches, making sure not to overcrowd the pan.

6. Cook the potato kebabs for about 3-4 minutes on each side, or until they are golden brown and crispy.

7. Remove the Potato Kebabs (Kartoflu Kebab) from the skillet and place them on a plate lined with paper towels to drain any excess oil.

Spinach Casserole

Servings: 4-6 Time: 45 minutes

Ingredients:

- 1 lb fresh spinach, washed and chopped
- 1 onion, finely chopped
- 2 cloves garlic, minced
- 1 cup cottage cheese
- 1 cup shredded mozzarella cheese
- 1/4 cup grated Parmesan cheese
- 1/4 cup breadcrumbs
- 2 tablespoons olive oil
- Salt and pepper to taste
- Optional: red pepper flakes, chopped fresh herbs (such as parsley or basil)

Instructions:

1. Preheat your oven to 375°F (190°C).
2. In a large skillet, heat the olive oil over medium heat. Add the finely chopped onion and minced garlic. Cook until the onion is translucent and the garlic is fragrant, about 5 minutes.

3. Add the chopped fresh spinach to the skillet. Cook until the spinach is wilted and cooked down, about 3-4 minutes. Remove from heat and let cool slightly.

4. In a large bowl, combine the cooked spinach mixture, cottage cheese, shredded mozzarella cheese, grated Parmesan cheese, breadcrumbs, salt, and pepper. Mix well to combine all the ingredients.

5. Transfer the spinach mixture to a greased casserole dish, spreading it out evenly.

6. Optional: Sprinkle red pepper flakes and chopped fresh herbs over the top for added flavor and garnish.

7. Bake the Spinach Casserole in the preheated oven for about 25-30 minutes, or until the top is golden brown and bubbly.

8. Remove the casserole from the oven and let it cool for a few minutes before serving.

DESSERTS

Walnut Baklava

Servings: 24 pieces Time: 1 hour 30 minutes

Ingredients:

- 1 package (16 oz) phyllo dough, thawed according to package instructions
- 1 cup unsalted butter, melted
- 2 cups walnuts, finely chopped
- 1 cup granulated sugar
- 1 teaspoon ground cinnamon
- 1/2 teaspoon ground cloves
- 1 cup water
- 1 cup honey

- 1 teaspoon vanilla extract
- Optional: whole cloves or cinnamon sticks for garnish

Instructions:

1. Preheat your oven to 350°F (175°C). Grease a 9x13-inch baking dish with melted butter.
2. In a bowl, combine the finely chopped walnuts, granulated sugar, ground cinnamon, and ground cloves. Mix well and set aside.
3. Unroll the thawed phyllo dough and cover it with a damp towel to prevent it from drying out.
4. Place one sheet of phyllo dough into the greased baking dish and brush it with melted butter. Repeat with another sheet of phyllo dough, brushing each layer with butter, until you have used about half of the phyllo sheets.
5. Sprinkle half of the walnut mixture evenly over the buttered phyllo layers in the baking dish.
6. Continue layering the remaining phyllo sheets on top of the walnut mixture, brushing each sheet with melted butter.
7. Sprinkle the remaining walnut mixture evenly over the top layer of phyllo dough.

8. Use a sharp knife to cut the baklava into diamond or square-shaped pieces.

9. Bake the Walnut Baklava in the preheated oven for about 45-50 minutes, or until golden brown and crisp.

10. While the baklava is baking, prepare the syrup. In a saucepan, combine the water, honey, and vanilla extract. Bring the mixture to a boil, then reduce the heat and simmer for about 10 minutes, stirring occasionally.

11. Remove the baklava from the oven and immediately pour the hot syrup evenly over the hot baklava. Let the baklava cool and absorb the syrup for several hours or overnight.

12. Optional: Garnish each piece of baklava with a whole clove or cinnamon stick before serving.

Gata (Armenian Sweet Bread)

Servings: 8-10 Time: 2 hours

Ingredients:

For the Dough:

- 4 cups all-purpose flour
- 1/2 cup granulated sugar
- 1/2 teaspoon salt
- 1 tablespoon active dry yeast
- 1 cup warm milk
- 1/2 cup unsalted butter, melted
- 2 large eggs
- 1 teaspoon vanilla extract

For the Filling:

- 1 cup unsalted butter, softened
- 1 cup granulated sugar
- 2 cups finely ground walnuts

For the Egg Wash:

- 1 egg yolk
- 1 tablespoon milk

Instructions:

1. In a large mixing bowl, combine the warm milk and yeast. Let it sit for about 5 minutes until foamy.

2. Add the melted butter, sugar, salt, eggs, and vanilla extract to the yeast mixture. Mix well.

3. Gradually add the flour to the wet ingredients, stirring until a soft dough forms. Knead the dough on a floured surface for about 5-7 minutes until smooth and elastic.

4. Place the dough in a greased bowl, cover with a kitchen towel, and let it rise in a warm place for about 1 hour or until doubled in size.

5. While the dough is rising, prepare the filling by mixing the softened butter, sugar, and finely ground walnuts in a bowl until well combined.

6. Preheat your oven to 350°F (175°C). Grease a baking sheet or line it with parchment paper.

7. Punch down the risen dough and divide it into two equal portions. Roll out each portion into a rectangle about 1/4 inch thick.

8. Spread half of the filling evenly over one of the rolled-out dough rectangles, leaving a small border around the edges.

9. Carefully roll up the dough from one of the long sides, forming a log. Repeat the same process with the other portion of dough and filling.

10. Place the two filled dough logs side by side on the prepared baking sheet, forming a braid by twisting them together gently.

11. In a small bowl, whisk together the egg yolk and milk to make the egg wash. Brush the egg wash over the top of the Gata.

12. Bake the Gata in the preheated oven for about 30-35 minutes, or until golden brown and cooked through.

13. Remove the Gata from the oven and let it cool on a wire rack before slicing and serving.

Rice Pudding (Sutlac)

Servings: 6-8 Time: 1 hour 30 minutes

Ingredients:

- 1/2 cup short-grain white rice
- 4 cups whole milk
- 1/2 cup granulated sugar
- 1/4 teaspoon salt
- 1 teaspoon vanilla extract
- 2 tablespoons cornstarch
- 1/4 cup cold water
- Ground cinnamon for garnish

Instructions:

1. Rinse the rice under cold water until the water runs clear. Drain well.
2. In a large saucepan, combine the rinsed rice, whole milk, granulated sugar, salt, and vanilla extract. Stir well to combine.
3. Bring the mixture to a boil over medium-high heat, stirring frequently to prevent the rice from sticking to the bottom of the pan.

4. Reduce the heat to low and let the rice pudding simmer gently, stirring occasionally, for about 30-35 minutes or until the rice is cooked and the mixture has thickened to a pudding-like consistency.

5. In a small bowl, dissolve the cornstarch in the cold water to create a slurry.

6. Gradually add the cornstarch slurry to the simmering rice pudding, stirring continuously until the pudding thickens further, about 5-7 minutes.

7. Remove the saucepan from heat and let the rice pudding cool slightly.

8. Divide the rice pudding into serving bowls or ramekins.

9. Cover the surface of each serving with plastic wrap to prevent a skin from forming, if desired.

10. Chill the Rice Pudding (Sutlac) in the refrigerator for at least 1 hour or until cold and set.

11. Before serving, sprinkle ground cinnamon over the top of each serving for garnish.

Apricot and Nut Bars

Servings: 12 bars Time: 1 hour

Ingredients:

For the Crust:

- 1 1/2 cups all-purpose flour
- 1/2 cup granulated sugar
- 1/4 teaspoon salt
- 1/2 cup unsalted butter, cold and cubed
- 1 large egg yolk
- 1 teaspoon vanilla extract

For the Filling:

- 1 cup dried apricots, chopped
- 1/2 cup water
- 1/4 cup honey
- 1/2 cup chopped nuts (such as almonds, walnuts, or pecans)
- 1/4 cup shredded coconut (optional)
- 1 tablespoon lemon juice

Instructions:

1. Preheat your oven to 350°F (175°C). Grease or line a 9x9-inch baking pan with parchment paper, leaving some overhang for easy removal.

2. In a food processor or a large bowl, combine the all-purpose flour, granulated sugar, and salt for the crust. Add the cold cubed butter and pulse or cut in using a pastry cutter until the mixture resembles coarse crumbs.

3. Add the egg yolk and vanilla extract to the mixture. Pulse or mix until the dough comes together and forms a ball. If the dough seems too dry, add a tablespoon of cold water.

4. Press the dough evenly into the bottom of the prepared baking pan to form the crust. Use the back of a spoon or your hands to smooth it out.

5. In a saucepan, combine the chopped dried apricots, water, honey, chopped nuts, shredded coconut (if using), and lemon juice for the filling. Bring the mixture to a simmer over medium heat, stirring occasionally.

6. Cook the filling for about 10-15 minutes or until the apricots are softened and the mixture has thickened slightly. Remove from heat and let it cool slightly.

7. Spread the apricot and nut filling evenly over the crust in the baking pan.

8. Bake the Apricot and Nut Bars in the preheated oven for about 25-30 minutes or until the crust is golden brown and the filling is set.

9. Remove the bars from the oven and let them cool completely in the pan on a wire rack.

10. Once cooled, use the parchment paper overhang to lift the bars out of the pan. Place them on a cutting board and cut into squares or bars.

11. Store the Apricot and Nut Bars in an airtight container at room temperature for up to a week.

Honey Cake (Tatik)

Servings: 12 slices Time: 1 hour 30 minutes

Ingredients:

For the Cake:

- 2 cups all-purpose flour
- 1 teaspoon baking powder
- 1/2 teaspoon baking soda
- 1/2 teaspoon ground cinnamon
- 1/4 teaspoon ground cloves
- 1/4 teaspoon ground nutmeg
- 1/4 teaspoon salt
- 1/2 cup unsalted butter, softened
- 1 cup granulated sugar
- 3 large eggs
- 1 teaspoon vanilla extract
- 1 cup plain yogurt
- 1/4 cup honey

For the Honey Glaze:

- 1/4 cup honey
- 1 tablespoon water

Instructions:

1. Preheat your oven to 350°F (175°C). Grease and flour a 9x13-inch baking pan.

2. In a medium bowl, whisk together the all-purpose flour, baking powder, baking soda, ground cinnamon, ground cloves, ground nutmeg, and salt. Set aside.

3. In a large mixing bowl, cream together the softened unsalted butter and granulated sugar until light and fluffy.

4. Add the eggs one at a time, beating well after each addition. Stir in the vanilla extract.

5. Gradually add the dry flour mixture to the wet ingredients, alternating with the plain yogurt, beginning and ending with the flour mixture. Mix until well combined.

6. Stir in the honey until evenly incorporated into the batter.

7. Pour the batter into the prepared baking pan and spread it out evenly.

8. Bake the Honey Cake (Tatik) in the preheated oven for about 30-35 minutes or until a toothpick inserted into the center comes out clean.

9. While the cake is baking, prepare the honey glaze. In a small saucepan, combine the honey and water. Heat over

low heat until the honey is melted and the mixture is smooth. Remove from heat and set aside.

10. Once the cake is done, remove it from the oven and let it cool in the pan for about 10 minutes.

11. Use a toothpick or skewer to poke holes all over the top of the cake. Pour the honey glaze evenly over the warm cake, allowing it to seep into the holes.

12. Let the Honey Cake cool completely in the pan on a wire rack before slicing and serving.

Walnut Cookies (Kurabiye)

Servings: 24 cookies Time: 45 minutes

Ingredients:

- 1 cup walnuts, finely chopped
- 1 cup unsalted butter, softened
- 1/2 cup powdered sugar
- 1 teaspoon vanilla extract
- 2 cups all-purpose flour
- 1/4 teaspoon salt
- Additional powdered sugar for dusting

Instructions:

1. Preheat your oven to 350°F (175°C). Line a baking sheet with parchment paper.
2. In a mixing bowl, cream together the softened unsalted butter and powdered sugar until light and fluffy.
3. Add the vanilla extract and mix until well combined.
4. Gradually add the all-purpose flour and salt to the butter mixture, mixing until a dough forms.
5. Fold in the finely chopped walnuts until evenly distributed throughout the dough.

6. Take small portions of the dough and roll them into balls, about 1 inch in diameter.

7. Place the cookie balls on the prepared baking sheet, spacing them about 1 inch apart.

8. Use a fork to gently press down on each cookie ball, creating a crisscross pattern on the top.

9. Bake the Walnut Cookies in the preheated oven for about 12-15 minutes or until the edges are golden brown.

10. Remove the cookies from the oven and let them cool on the baking sheet for a few minutes.

11. While still warm, dust the tops of the cookies with powdered sugar.

12. Transfer the Walnut Cookies to a wire rack to cool completely before serving.

Fruit Compote

Servings: 4 Time: 20 minutes

Ingredients:

- 2 cups mixed fresh or frozen fruits (such as berries, peaches, plums, or apples), chopped
- 1/4 cup water
- 2-3 tablespoons granulated sugar (adjust according to taste)
- 1 teaspoon lemon juice
- Optional: cinnamon stick, vanilla extract, or other spices for flavoring

Instructions:

1. In a saucepan, combine the chopped mixed fruits, water, granulated sugar, and lemon juice.
2. If using, add a cinnamon stick or other spices for additional flavor.
3. Bring the mixture to a gentle simmer over medium heat, stirring occasionally.
4. Let the fruit simmer for about 10-15 minutes or until the fruits are tender and the liquid has slightly thickened to form a syrupy consistency.

5. Remove the saucepan from heat and let the fruit compote cool slightly.

6. If desired, stir in a splash of vanilla extract for added flavor.

7. Serve the Fruit Compote warm or chilled, either on its own as a dessert or topping for yogurt, ice cream, pancakes, or oatmeal.

8. Store any leftover fruit compote in an airtight container in the refrigerator for up to a week.

Sweet Cheese Pastry (Ghurabiye)

Servings: 16 pastries Time: 1 hour 30 minutes

Ingredients:

For the Pastry Dough:

- 2 cups all-purpose flour
- 1/2 cup unsalted butter, softened
- 1/4 cup granulated sugar
- 1/4 teaspoon salt
- 1/4 cup cold water
- 1 teaspoon vanilla extract

For the Sweet Cheese Filling:

- 1 cup ricotta cheese or farmer's cheese
- 1/4 cup powdered sugar
- 1 egg yolk
- 1/2 teaspoon vanilla extract
- Optional: ground cinnamon or nutmeg for flavor

For Assembly:

- 1 egg, beaten (for egg wash)
- Powdered sugar for dusting

Instructions:

1. Preheat your oven to 350°F (175°C). Line a baking sheet with parchment paper.

2. In a mixing bowl, combine the softened unsalted butter, granulated sugar, and salt. Mix until creamy and well combined.

3. Gradually add the all-purpose flour to the butter mixture, mixing until a crumbly dough forms.

4. Add the cold water and vanilla extract to the dough. Mix until the dough comes together into a smooth ball. If needed, add more water, a tablespoon at a time, until the dough is cohesive.

5. In a separate bowl, prepare the sweet cheese filling by combining the ricotta cheese (or farmer's cheese), powdered sugar, egg yolk, and vanilla extract. Add ground cinnamon or nutmeg if desired for extra flavor.

6. Divide the pastry dough into 16 equal portions. Roll each portion into a ball.

7. Flatten each dough ball into a small disc using your palms or a rolling pin, creating a small indentation in the center for the filling.

8. Place a spoonful of the sweet cheese filling into the center of each dough disc.

9. Fold the edges of the dough over the filling, pinching them together to seal and form a ball with the filling enclosed inside.

10. Place the filled pastries on the prepared baking sheet.

11. Brush the tops of the pastries with beaten egg for a golden finish.

12. Bake the Sweet Cheese Pastries in the preheated oven for about 25-30 minutes or until golden brown and cooked through.

13. Remove the pastries from the oven and let them cool on a wire rack.

14. Dust the cooled pastries with powdered sugar before serving.

Nut Brittle

Servings: About 12 servings Time: 30 minutes

Ingredients:

- 1 cup granulated sugar
- 1/2 cup water
- 1/2 cup light corn syrup
- 1/4 teaspoon salt
- 1 tablespoon unsalted butter
- 1 teaspoon vanilla extract
- 1 cup mixed nuts (such as almonds, peanuts, or cashews), roughly chopped
- 1 teaspoon baking soda

Instructions:

1. Prepare a baking sheet by lining it with parchment paper or greasing it lightly with butter. Set it aside.
2. In a heavy-bottomed saucepan, combine the granulated sugar, water, corn syrup, and salt. Stir well to combine.
3. Place the saucepan over medium-high heat and bring the mixture to a boil. Stir occasionally until the sugar has dissolved completely.

4. Once the mixture reaches a boil, insert a candy thermometer into the saucepan. Continue to cook the syrup without stirring until it reaches 300°F (hard crack stage).

5. Remove the saucepan from heat and quickly stir in the unsalted butter and vanilla extract until well combined.

6. Add the chopped mixed nuts to the syrup mixture and stir quickly to coat the nuts evenly.

7. Sprinkle the baking soda over the nut mixture and stir again. The mixture will bubble and foam up.

8. Pour the hot nut brittle mixture onto the prepared baking sheet, spreading it out into an even layer with a spatula.

9. Let the nut brittle cool and harden at room temperature for about 30 minutes to 1 hour.

10. Once the brittle has completely cooled and hardened, break it into pieces using your hands or a kitchen mallet.

11. Store the Nut Brittle in an airtight container at room temperature. It can last for several weeks if stored properly.

Date Rolls (Rahat)

Servings: About 20 date rolls Time: 30 minutes

Ingredients:

- 1 cup pitted dates
- 1/2 cup nuts (such as almonds, walnuts, or pistachios), finely chopped
- 1 tablespoon unsalted butter
- 1/2 teaspoon ground cinnamon
- Optional: desiccated coconut or powdered sugar for coating

Instructions:

1. In a food processor, combine the pitted dates, chopped nuts, unsalted butter, and ground cinnamon. Pulse the mixture until it forms a sticky and uniform paste.
2. Scoop out the date and nut mixture onto a piece of parchment paper or a clean surface.
3. Divide the mixture into small portions and roll each portion into a cylindrical shape, forming date rolls.
4. Optional: Roll the date rolls in desiccated coconut or powdered sugar for coating, if desired.
5. Place the date rolls on a serving dish or tray.

6. Chill the Date Rolls (Rahat) in the refrigerator for about 30 minutes to firm up.

MEASURES

1. **Volume Conversions:**
   - 1 cup = 240 milliliters
   - 1 tablespoon = 15 milliliters
   - 1 teaspoon = 5 milliliters
   - 1 fluid ounce = 30 milliliters
2. **Weight Conversions:**
   - 1 ounce = 28 grams
   - 1 pound = 453 grams
   - 1 kilogram = 2.2 pounds
3. **Temperature Conversions:**
   - Celsius to Fahrenheit: $F = (C \times 9/5) + 32$
   - Fahrenheit to Celsius: $C = (F - 32) \times 5/9$
4. **Length Conversions:**
   - 1 inch = 2.54 centimeters

- 1 foot = 30.48 centimeters

- 1 meter = 39.37 inches

5. **Common Ingredient Conversions:**

- 1 stick of butter = 1/2 cup = 113 grams

- 1 cup of flour = 120 grams

- 1 cup of sugar = 200 grams

6. **Oven Temperature Conversions:**

- Gas Mark 1 = 275°F = 140°C

- Gas Mark 2 = 300°F = 150°C

- Gas Mark 4 = 350°F = 180°C

- Gas Mark 6 = 400°F = 200°C

- Gas Mark 8 = 450°F = 230°C

Made in United States
Orlando, FL
01 July 2025

62535150R00069